THE NEW WORLD

PRINCETON SERIES OF CONTEMPORARY POETS
Susan Stewart, series editor

For other titles in the Princeton Series of Contemporary Poets see the end of this volume.

THE NEW WORLD

Infinitesimal Epics

Anthony Carelli

PRINCETON UNIVERSITY PRESS
Princeton and Oxford

Published by Princeton University Press
41 William Street, Princeton, New Jersey 08540
6 Oxford Street, Woodstock, Oxfordshire OX20 1TR

press.princeton.edu

Library of Congress Cataloging-in-Publication Data

Names: Carelli, Anthony, 1979- author.
Title: The new world : Infinitesimal epics / Anthony Carelli.
Description: Princeton : Princeton University Press, [2021] | Series: Princeton series of contemporary poets
Identifiers: LCCN 2021004422 | ISBN 9780691218809 (hardback) | ISBN 9780691218793 (paperback) | ISBN 9780691218816 (ebook)
Subjects: LCGFT: Poetry.
Classification: LCC PS3603.A736 N49 2021 | DDC 811/.6--dc23
LC record available at https://lccn.loc.gov/2021004422

British Library Cataloging-in-Publication Data is available

Editorial: Anne Savarese and James Collier
Production Editorial: Ellen Foos
Text Design: Pamela Schnitter
Jacket/Cover Design: Pamela Schnitter
Production: Erin Suydam
Publicity: Jodi Price and Amy Stewart
Copyeditor: Jodi Beder

Jacket/cover image: George Shiras, "Three white-tailed deer, Michigan" (ca. 1893–1898). Earliest nighttime flash photograph taken in Michigan © National Geographic Creative Archives

This book has been composed in Adobe Garamond Pro and Scala Sans

Printed on acid-free paper. ∞

Printed in the United States of America

10 9 8 7 6 5 4 3 2 1

For Augustine

Contents

THE NEW WORLD

Proem: The Ultrasound Technician Tells Us You Can Hear Our Voices

My, my little Columbus,
adrift at sea in utero,
you're already reaching
for worlds to come.

shadow: lima bean, hawk
beak, bowsprit, it's you
steering to face what booms
across your Indian Ocean.

more peaceable,
less maniacal?
The spirit invoked
homes to only

—Who would dare?
Pilgrim, distant
listener, be it me
or be it thunder,

thicketed wood . . .
I step out to meet you,
to sound on the shore
for which you are bound.

Tracing the screen,
more inkblot than portrait,
we draw what is
from what is

A disenstoried man
on disenstoried land,
shouldn't I open with
some cute synecdoche

gilded horizons.
Couldn't I—shouldn't I—
soften what I shape
by shifting sounds?

you hear beasts
of unknown order.
Savage to you,
I hesitate in this

Please land gently.
And listen and
listen and listen
and stay.

I

Plato: *But, I take it, if he had genuine knowledge of the things he imitates he would far rather devote himself to real things than to the imitation of them, and would endeavor to leave after him many noble deeds and works as memorials of himself, and would be more eager to be the theme of praise, than the praiser*

-but-

Dante Jokes in Peshtigo

Scene: the dark wood. Our two heroes, voluntary exiles, already having
second thoughts, search their imaginations: What do people do out here?

I mean for *fun*. Our first night away, at a cottage near the Peshtigo River,
we sit on the screen porch after dinner, watching the woods get darker.

"It's the gloaming," I say. "That's what we call this in literature—
the sun is dead but not yet fallen." As soon as the words take flight

I see them flap, flop, and fall. So do you. "Hmm," you sweetly sing back,
"that's not *altogether* unexciting, Poet."

Your chuckle flies
loop-de-loops and
disappears.

A great quip comes to mind: "Yes, well
wasn't it Dante, in Venice, in 1321,

who said *It can take a man a day or two to settle into his vacation?*"
. . . I await your appreciative gasp . . . "You know because he'd been

banished from Florence for twenty years by then, so . . ."

. . . crickets . . .

The dark of the wood is settling now like tarnish on gold, like an aging
of the lower light spraying through the old growth (mostly white pine,

I learned today). The midriffs of their trunks—what all can be seen
from the forest floor to roof's edge—are blushing, then plum purple,

now turning brown between buckles of twilight. "You're glowing,"
you say to me, and so there comes and goes a moment when the air's

bright ochre rises in briefly warmer hues, sweeping its robes across
the grassy saucer of a clearing, and through the porch screens

of this rental, the only cottage for what must be miles around. Another
titter
and our   "Oh God. Aren't you starving?" We both say *starving*
infini-   just like that. It's a prehistoric hunger joke we re-
tesimal
epic   prised after dinner, after we nibbled our seven butter
has   crackers, and nibbled blaze squares of strange cheddar
up and
flown   and nibbled our ears, one each, of pale-kernel sweet corn.
away.   It's all we packed to eat, not enough, but we found

such failings funny: "Really, love, this *is* a perfect dinner." "Perfect for
a mouse starving to death in winter." *A strange humor, ours, we don't*

think, this unfunny humor, who, though we mind it no longer, goes
echoing out there somewhere, echoing darker. Where? To whom?

There must be whole worlds elsewhere for the unthought thoughts
that have flown—like Shouldn't a story so humble have ended already?

Deep twilight now, the birds begin to speak, sweet singing

in the bellies of trees, voices in shadows and a few last lit leaves—
all a bit troubled, or so it seems: *Cuckoo . . . Chick-a-dee . . . Phoebe*
                                      so emphatic.
I tell you, though, my better listener, at the beck   *Cuckoo . . .*
of the call, in the song of these shadows who   *kill-will . . .*
                                        Chuck-deer . . .
sing their own names, what flashes to my mind   *Koo . . .*
is fire, the Peshtigo Fire that I learned so little about

from the single laminated page left squared to the corners
of the kitchen counter to welcome weekend guests like us:

Peshtigo Rose Getaway Rental
and Deer Hunting Lodge

Emergency Numbers . . .   Local Attractions . . .   and The Peshtigo Fire . . .
In these woods, the paragraph begins . . .   October 8, 1871 . . .
1,500 people . . .   2,500 people . . .   Cold front strong
winds . . .   fire whirl . . .   because of drought . . .   like a crema-
torium . . .   Mile-high flame . . .   Peshtigo Paradigm . . .
studied by American and British . . .   Legacy . . .   firebombing
of Dresden . . .   such incendiary devices . . .   firebombing
of Tokyo . . .   conditions absolutely perfect . . .

Well, that's a bit far-fetched: the Peshtigo Paradigm? Doubtful.
Some bored Peshtigoan must be dying for attention. I said this all
                                                    to no one
But you, better listener, won't you hear how   in the kitchen
these lines, as if spoken by shadow, come   back then.

echoing back to me now? Won't you hear in these lines that fail me
a cruelty, my cruelty, I, who am not altogether non-native to this place?

Cuckoo,   Still, I lift these lesser lines to you. When was it, love,
Whip-will,   on this first night away from our stories in the city,
Chick-a-
dee, Koo . . . when did we slip beyond hunger? (For one does slip
              beyond hunger.) And down to what rung slips

the un-hungry soul? We don't think these thoughts, either, as now
"Shh. Listen . . . Whippoorwill!" you whisper. And as dark sprawls in

around us, as the lantern light, our inside light, now thickens
on the screens, screening off any glimpse of the woods, we hear—

far off at first, then closer coming, then brushing by—not that bird
whose name you called, but the exile and his underworld guide,

the pilgrim whose seminal song encircles us all in our own unheard conversations. This bewildered question banks in the pitch, pumps

its wings once, and glides back now to have its answer. Here, a hoot among shadows' many ears, this one-word song, the Commedian's:

Who?
Who were you once?
Who are you now?
Who?
Who?
Who?

The Buck

It all happened so quickly.
I'm afraid there isn't much to tell.
I was back in Wisconsin
visiting my parents,
both retired already,
both healthy at the time.
One evening before dinner
I went for a jog, my usual jog
on the pine woods loop
behind the sewage plant
not far from their house,
and there was the buck.

Ugh, was it hot that summer!
A wet heat, really miserable.
Even Mister McCarthy,
our most *denying* neighbor,
allowed that "Well, things
really do seem warmer than ever
this September."
This was some days later,
when he "just thought" to drop by
and "just happened," he said,
to bring a bundle
of his teriyaki venison jerky,
truly the world's best,
a Get Well gift for me.

But here I wander
ahead of myself.
I had just crossed the marsh
on the bouncy wood bridge.
I'd come sailing through
those waves of mosquitoes—
there must be ten thousand,

they seem to always be there
flying, flying to nowhere,
more mosquitoes than air—
and then up the marsh bank
where the trail is loose sand
and your feet slip back
and I stopped.

A whitetail deer,
a tremendous buck,
ten points, twelve maybe.
His flank walled off the way,
ten yards between us.
His rump was set toward me,
his shoulders angled away,
a rather nonchalant pose
I might have sensed,
if not for the snapped-up white
of his tail, the deep still lake
of his stare, the spiked ears,
the antlers.

He took me in
but went right on chewing,
more concerned, I gathered,
about the leaf he'd plucked
from the bright shoots dallied
on the edge of the trail
than about the sound I'd been
or the man I'd become.
Then, the muscles flickered,
if such can be seen.
The lines of the buck
had darkened, retraced
just once in pencil
in the low gold sunlight.

How lovely running makes
the evening feel. Moments ago
this is what I'd been thinking,
this or some other empty line;
maybe *The air as cool as skin*
so as it swishes past
I feel the arms and thighs
of something unfeeling, ever-gentle,

some being un-bodied
and everywhere.

 While, later,
after the buck, I recall
what there was to recall:
that I looked at the eyes,
only the eyes,
a still heart lake, water onyx;
and that the buck knew only
to look back at me.
What did he see?

When I fled through
the grasses and back
along the bouncy bridge
I ran with the buck's eyes
like faint imperfections
on every last frame
of the film of my mind.
And so through those eyes—
or beyond them, rather,
behind their black blots—
I see what I can. It happens
so quickly.

The snow belly flashed
as the buck reared up,
the four groins stretched
and the front hooves struck
painless quick punches:
my wrist and my shoulder
my cheek and my spine.
"No, no, hey, no, no,"
I recall calling out.
I looked at the buck's eyes
but saw only through.
Then the tips of three antlers
slipped into my skin,
slid painless in triceps,
hamstring, and back meat,
bone drumming bone.

Pain: no pain at all.
I was well past the bridge then,

then back on the road.
And what came next
came clearer than whatever
had come.
        I was home again,
yet running still toward home,
I was back on the sandy path.
I'd spooked from the tree there
whose cover I'd sought
and who never cried out
as the last of the hoofpunches
pummeled arrhythmic.
For a time I was walking
and the blood was all sweat
in a slick down my flank.
My shorts were soaked.
I'd be just fine. My mother
was bowing like a birch tree,
bowing down toward me,
bone-eyed, but not crying.

The buck bounded off then
as any deer ought to,
into the woods: still there,
the milk-brown body,
smaller then, then gone,
gone but still flashing,
the tail still white, white,
a heatless light, the pale of
ashes shadowing snow.

For who-knows-how-long-then
I lay like this on the kitchen floor.
The volunteer ambulance was
running slowly. I was queasy,
dizzy. Funny, the world was
spinning, as we say *literally*.
But hadn't it always been spinning?
Some days later my mother
recalls for me how calm
I'd been, how composed;

how carefully I'd told
her the story,
yet, how inconsolably
I'd babbled on and on and on,
on details that seemed
insignificant to her:
the fate of the new
kitchen tile, for one,
my good mother's kitchen floor—
it was catching the worst
of my blackening blood.
The tile was brand-new
and pure white to boot,
a no-shoes floor,
a white as pure as light
on the truth of the matter
at hand, this light
unimaginably white
and indescribably cold.

Charlie at Full Speed

Sure, Anna Belle put it best: "Give us more Charlie at full speed."
    Yet, on that day we can't forget
  nothing much happened. Though Boston was simply ablaze,
    Leeore had proposed a game of bocce

and so his father, Howie, dove deep in the closet to scare up some
    sun hats. The only one that fit me
  was a chartreuse affair with an acre of floppy brim. It made a pale
    flower of me. "Photo-worthy,"

said Rivka, adding "Anthony, really, it's a bad architectural
    experiment on your head." And taking
  play pity, her hands scaled the scaffold to the cornices, rebending
    the saturnine rim—but I digress . . .

Charlie at Full Speed. It being our very first day together—Anna
    Belle, Anthony, Rivka and Howie
  with Leeore the hub of our orbits, and being Howie and Rivka's
    first game of bocce, I'll call it

our inaugural day. So, in short: five of us, misfit hats, a park in
    Jamaica Plain, nothing much happened.
  Charlie, their greyhound, came too. A rescue, delicate, rather
    handsome, and placid, *glacially* placid—

until his flame-sharp head shot straight through Anna Belle's thighs.
    "Be polite, Charlie," said Howie;
  and Charlie was. Leashed, he loped, lay down, then loped on
    alongside us, as our underhand bowls

of blue and red balls so rarely very close to the pale "pallino" or "jack"
    led us up the park moraines
  and down through the kettles. To cool off we'd shade ourselves in
    the still warm craters of tree shade.

Then Charlie got loose . . . But, before that: some small talk. "I love your
    sunglasses." "Ah, good, Rivka.
  Nice toss." "Making a documentary about 26/11." "Charlie's the
    first greyhound I've ever known."

"How long in that apartment?" "I'll sit out the first round." "Hot as
    hell." "What do you teach, Rivka?"—
  and so on. Our small talk: it's barely built of language, a two stones'
    hit clicking not quite exchanging

anything. But isn't the ceasefire made of such material? And won't it
    get even smaller the smaller
  we're able to see? Charlie sighed and sighed and sighed. "Aw nuts I
    hit a rock er root er something"

as a red ball headed off squirrelly down the ravine. Then Charlie got
    loose. "Invented at the heights
  of the Roman Empire, the game of bocce . . ." boasted the wrinkled
    booklet dug up from the bottom

of the canvas tote. And yonder "NO DOGS OFF LEASH" hollered back
    a rust-lit Parks & Rec sign.
  He sighed and sighed. When the dog sighed I thought of that false
    friend sigh *ages and ages hence,*

the one prophesied by Robert Frost, that most misread exhalation
    and subsequent delusion of a nation,
  how less and less is insignificant, how more and more is
    insignificant, in the year the boys bombed

the marathon, in the year I resolved to txt fewer pix. And it may be
      beside the point, but, along the way,
   I might add, I'd been playing a fairly mean game of bocce, scoring
      five to your three, your one,

and your zero. "Ladies and gentlemen, ladies and gentlemen, may I
      have your attention, please. Move
   aside. Now observe: the poet will show you just how it's done."
      And then, "You're dead, Carelli."

That was Leeore, as if just pretending the win means the world.
      Leashed, he loped, lay down,
   then loped on alongside us. Then Charlie got loose. We all sure
      got along. The brute heat helped.

"Quick look at Charlie." The headline of the local rag that morning
      read simply "Baked Bean."
   That got chuckles all around. Across the field: a tessellation, every
      shape a Charlie, Charlie, Charlie

at full speed. An omega far off. "Watch the road." An arch or a line
      storm when close. Then dash,
   a teardrop, an oval over oval over oval, counter-clock. "Charlie,
      no." "Watch the road." And so—

"Charlie, no"—the five of us sallied forth, flying, fingers of debris,
      sailing out centrifugally
   across the paw-drawn ruts in the field of a greyhound's mind.
      "Poor Charlie," someone said.

"Poor Charlie." Though nothing much happened. By then the
      greyhound had stopped. Charlie,
   now still, extended his throat just a little, just enough so his
      flickered tongue could taste the skin

of the salt city now spinning above. Then, quite close to Rivka,
    Charlie sat down, knelt down, then lay
  across his red leash. He looked at none of us. He entertained no
    prayer. He breathed, breathed,

breathed again, then set down his throat on the dirt. Charlie at full
    speed: like a sand-white shard
  the eye catches only obliquely, watches let go as an Earth-blue cup
    shatters, preternaturally slow . . .

"Whose toss?" "Your toss, Anna Belle." And she said, "Just you wait,"
    then scattered the rest of us
  with the best ball of the day. And there came a "Hey! Hey!" from the
    hilltop. Three silhouettes, not friendly,

wriggly, obviously drunk. Wormy arms lifted three black cans of
    black beer in the impure white sky,
  saluting us—who, when seen from such a distance, must also
    resemble mere shades of ourselves;

or the enemy tribe. Still, I get the sense whenever I tell this story,
    that, had those phantoms not been
  keeping watch, we'd've lost our hold on the dry slope, and slipped
    right out of Massachusetts.

Octet 9

Скажи мне, чертежник пустыни,
Арабских песков геометр,
Ужели безудержность линий
Сильнее, чем дующий ветр?
— Меня не касается трепет
Его иудейских забот —
Он опыт из лепета лепит
И лепет из опыта пьет.

from Osip Mandelstam's "Moscow Notebooks"

Octet 9

Tell me, great desert dreamer,
geometer of empty Arabian sands:
will the capricious wit of your lines
really withstand the worry of the winds?

      "That concerns me not, friend—
      such Judaic chaos in the worried winds."
      Whatever blowing molds a land out of babble
            drinks from the babble of that land.

from Osip Mandelstam's "Moscow Notebooks"

Octet 9

I can't shake this vision: Ypsilanti, Michigan, the barefooted fella strolls
    away from the Walmart parking lot as I crawl along in my old
    Toyota. One wonders how a man comes to walk where there's no
    sidewalk, no footpath, no earth. To cross the bridge over I-94 he
    takes his chances in the pinch where the tires of big rigs have
    blackened the concrete guardrail. The story goes nowhere; there's
    nowhere to go.

I don't know the man from Adam; saw him just that once and I can't seem
    to shake him, nor do I really have reason to try. This pilgrim
    bound to be eternal, as out-of-place within the mind as was a man
    upon that slab, that mythless stretch of road. How *plain* the old
    vision grows—biblically so. And I recall nothing else about him;
    well, except his hair, a tar-black slick so immaculately combed;
    and his bare feet dingy as mechanics' rags, like the
    nevermore-white of the late May snow.

from Osip Mandelstam's "Moscow Notebooks"

Where the Green Ants Dream

These nights in the desert of our kitchen are so very cold that even a
    literary man
    isn't much in the mood for a story. No matter. Maestro Herzog
    thumbs

his deck of picture cards, and—*Action!*—just like that our man comes
    around.
    First frame: out of nothing, in the beginning an ever-materializing
    twister

licks the outback. Next come the sandy concussions, blast plume
    treetops
    sand shower leaves: one pop, two pop, darkening the screen,
    three pop, four.

The mining company's conveyor machines are long past drunk,
    vomiting rocks.
    Ooh, the sound of a didgeridoo! Now, who knows where that
    bulldozer goes,

but three Aborigines sit in the way. By now of course I'm hooked.
    What can a man do
    to undo what's undone? Well, like any great story this one will be
    nothing

if not predictable. The Aborigines champion the land and, if
    necessary, fight back
    by loitering in the supermarket and cursing the white man
    obliquely, purely

in hearsay. You see, the green ants are dreaming; they must not be
    disturbed . . .
    Predictably the company lawyers conspire to bribe the tribe. Less
        predictably

the clincher is a twin-prop airplane. Then, for whom is this
    predictable?
    The tribesmen value not the machine's most exquisite attribute,
        the very fact

of its flightworthiness, but rather the pellucid powers of its
    immaculate skin.
    And what color skin? What do you suppose? What color suits
        their insect cosmos?

Uneasily, I watch the Aborigines lay skittish hands on the belly
    of this impassive giant.
    Then I wrest control of the symbol by recalling *Fitzcarraldo*
    (same director).

The enterprising Fitzcarraldo and his band of inimitable natives—
    the people
    of the Peruvian Amazon, in this case—once hoisted a steamship
    up and over

a jungle mountain in real life. It's famously not fake. The pulleys
    really tremble
    and the cables really break, dancing and dying under weight of
    the impossible.

Am I blessed tonight, then, that there's no Herzog to capture the grace
    with which I
    balance on the stool at our kitchen table, how my shoulders slope
    in genuflection,

how my eyes shimmer in the pool of my laptop screen, my movements
for a moment, as exquisite
as those of the extras, wholly indifferent to the camera? The ones
the director calls Campas

play the part even off screen, where, I hear, in servitude to Herzog,
they offered to murder
the maniac Fitzcarraldo (perhaps the world's finest actor),
murder him for real.

At the end of *Where the Green Ants Dream* there's a trial. By then I've
endeavored to pour
and finish myself a third brandy old-fashioned, and during the
proceedings chomp

the sandstone ice. The sound: deafening, pleasing. At a critical point,
in a silver suit,
there enters the courtroom an Aboriginal man who's heretofore
unseen.

The more—what's the word: *mainstream?*—Aborigines call this man
The Mute.
He's anything but. In fact, The Mute's are the world's last words
of a lost dialect.

So, though the man's solemn address is the sound of a throat, lips,
and tongue,
nobody understands his message—no more than one would that . . .
say . . . of chamber music.

Behold, then, how, minutes later, somewhere en route from the
bathroom across
the vast purple savannah, I catch the full weight of my body, thirty-five
years old,

as what inhale had hoisted an exhale let fall. I stop for a breather,
     luxuriating
  in every last taste of an Earth whose dust is aglitter with
     Aquafresh toothpaste.

Verily, then, in the hallway of our apartment I slip out edgewise,
     as a word
  might slip in, and it follows that I'm plucked by a homing pigeon . . .
     ten miles high . . .

I'm borne across the sandscape undevelopable, all blank but for
     those pale little
  pyramids—ant castles?—, the same desert across which the film's
     ethical hero walks

off the jobsite, strolling out in search of the even more impossible—
     or so we think we know
  for now. Conversely, as a kitten exploded from the crate is
     returned by its mother

I'm caught up in the gentle maw and lowered through clouds toward
     the pillows
  where I live. Here, the great myth, round trip, predictably returns
     our storyteller

to the world's tallest mountain, upon which this man does not live
     alone, returns me
  to the milk-smelling darkness of our bedroom, where I hear your
     voice: "Babe . . . ?"

"Yes, Love . . ." And there ends our day of mourning together—and apart—
     but for a few
  last errant sounds, sea breezes of your newest dreams, dreams
     of your mother still alive,

the sail ship sounds of your thighs swishing sheets. The old world that
  had risen into focus
 disappears underfoot as I'm set down upon it, awakening again,
  as I am now

as if forever, in real life, squinting down toward you, along
  the bright
 moon line broken by flippant lake water, silent, upon a peak near
  Milwaukee.

II

But, I take it, if he had genuine knowledge of the things he imitates he would far rather devote himself to real things than to the imitation of them, and would endeavor to leave after him many noble deeds and works as memorials of himself, and would be more eager to be the theme of praise, than the praiser.

- but -

Keats: *Then felt I like some watcher of the skies*
When a new planet swims into his ken;
Or like stout Cortez when with eagle eyes
He star'd at the Pacific—and all his men
Look'd at each other with a wild surmise—
Silent, upon a peak in Darien.

- but -

The New World

It's true: Pilgrim, for you it may be that nothing happens
anymore. That life is this going on all around

you all the time and nothing else. That this land
is blank land. This land is blank land, from California

to the unnamed island. That from an Apollo stair-
case you may leap each morning a moonwalker

to discover the plains of Kansas at last devoid
of evil men. That hallelujah now the cavalry

may ride at your command, crusading backward
through memory, their sword blades trued with

all we know now but couldn't know then. That
your warhorse's hammering head hits the source.

That who, you rightly ask, who are the savages now.
And true it may be that the whole of your light

shines forth in this darkening sky, the heaven
between the dot that ends this sentence and

the great cross heralding the next. That the in-
finitesimal is your new glory—and that indeed

there is glory in a certain kind of small. That in
the long night within your bones there hangs

the shard of a crescent moon. That we awaken—
who?—every morning in a tome of tomes of tomes.

That the great star's immense burning, so faintly
printed on a noontime flag, reminds us all that

it is so. That grace may await you nonetheless,
Pilgrim. That in this in-between breath, you may

find your rightful home, in these stories that no one
remembers that—without you—no one knows.

The New World

1932.
The Philippines.
The silver dirt path
disappearing in the woods
at the foot
of the fuzzy green hill.

The bronze little girl
my grandmother Ann
the bronze little girl
on a golden Schwinn.

	could she toe touch
Neither	peddles from the saddle
	if she sat

	sit in the saddle
nor	when she pedaled,
	even if she pedaled tippy-toe.

But the bronze little girl
like a chicken wing churning
up the fuzzy green hill
up the silver dirt path
up the golden Schwinn goes

and goes.
On the hilltop then

at the end of the road
the little bronze girl
let the golden Schwinn go,

for this   *Boxes, boxes neatly*
is what   *placed inside boxes,*
she saw: *street blocks gravel in a grid,*
                 tin roofs flashing,
                 airplane hangars over yonder
                 to the left
                 like open dark boxes:
                 wet and cool, rather
                 like holes in a painting,
                 like the dark in people's mouths;
                 and a green glittering,
                 a sprinkling of green
                 like pieces of a beer bottle
                 broken up in heaven—
                 those were the victory gardens;
                 and battleships like hills
                 full of buildings
                 in the harbor,
                 and the tiny sunfish sailboats
                 like bobbers
                 in the battleship waves,
                 their tiny flag sails
                 all white then black
                 white then black
                 on the dark ocean blue in
                 wind and milk waves.
                 And the palm trees . . .

                 And that's when I thought it
                 (still grandmother talking)
                 that's when I knew it!

I mean who could ever,
who in the world would ever imagine
this little me, here?

The Philippines,
in the middle of the ocean
on the fuzzy green hill . . .

No one sees me. No one sees me.
I must never forget I was here
for the rest of my life.

she retells this story
then forgets what she told
Today   and retells the same story again:
in Tempe,
Arizona   the golden Schwinn
the little bronze girl
my grandmother Ann.

Old Trees Wave

September 11th again. The old trees wave.
The old trees wave in the park across the way;
rather in the park sky above, forever blue today,
or wave in the frame of my office window, rather.
Down in the crosswalk, a nanny, or mother—or nanny
and mother, or how do you see she's a nanny?—or neither?
She pauses there with her wheelie bassinette, stopped in
the horns of morning traffic. Struck like me, she stares
up into the trees, the leaves, the static, her blouse
blooming an aluminum black. I'm afraid this
doesn't matter. The old trees waver.
They waver within themselves,
waver the same without,
and much to
the bewild-
erment of
everyone,
there is no
message. Not
until that wa-
vering word
breaks off,
sharp as
spear.

The New World

Sometimes
when I'm very angry,
but not sure about what
exactly, I become President
for a while—it helps to get me
through. Any President will do.
Ordinarily I'm a mild-mannered
fella, rather gentle of tongue—
an old man in spirit (or so my
old chums say), though even
chums become mere chum
in a mouth full of mouths
when I'm President.
Slurs, curses,
a flickering philoso-
phical snafu: this President can
say just about anything, and there's no telling when
he'll start. There's just something about this office that frees up
a man to be me. Thank you . . . Thank you . . . I didn't even know I had it
in me—honestly—not until we made me President . . . Or the story goes
this morning, as I hold court over buckets of clams at this open-air market.

A New Word

Nulla ignoranza mai con tanta guerra
mi fé desideroso di sapere,
se la memoria mia in ciò non erra,
quanta pareami allor, pensando, avere;

Out of sighs of a star now extinct, out of some unsound sound, this pale word was born so humbly, all but empty, yet it will, as un-willable as waters from the ocean floor, rise and crest with a speed all its own. Even what arises from the hoards of Homer, Chapman, Keats, and Cortez—or better said, Balboa—falls back as quickly as the Appalachian Mountains breaking and frothing and sucking back to the sea.

Now
as if
forever:

that sort of speed—and meanwhile, we, though we build upon its lines and farm upon its slopes, we may live and die and never feel this pale word tremble. Though, when we do, Pilgrim, we will tremble, too.

III

*But, I take it, if he had genuine knowledge of the things he imitates
he would far rather devote himself to real things than to the
imitation of them, and would endeavor to leave after him many
noble deeds and works as memorials of himself, and would be more
eager to be the theme of praise, than the praiser.*

- but -

*Then felt I like some watcher of the skies
When a new planet swims into his ken;
Or like stout Cortez when with eagle eyes
He star'd at the Pacific—and all his men
Look'd at each other with a wild surmise—
Silent, upon a peak in Darien.*

- but -

Mandelstam: *The signal waves of meaning vanish, having
completed their work; the more potent they are, the
more yielding, and the less inclined to linger.*

The New Horizons Spacecraft Speeds Past Pluto in What We May Call the Blink of an Eye

We explore because we are human
and we want to know.
                              —Stephen Hawking

Thank you,
little robot
that cannot stop

blinking by
a world
that no one

can live on;
through you
we glimpse—

or glow forth—
an image
of ourselves re-

perfected.
And we lose it
at once.

At the cusp
of illusion
it was us

not Pluto
you placed
in place,

so won-
derful, fun-
ny, and small.

Here, we listen.
There, your signal
fades out
in out-

er space . . .
In reaching
to know

never knowing
you plant us
again

inert
in the ethics
of dirt

like a tree
by the rivers
of water.

Country Canto

I was seventeen and working
in the fields that summer.
A seed corn job, not bad pay,
detasselling and rogueing mostly.
The fields were up near Oxford
up past the new penitentiary,
a three-hour drive both ways
so we'd get home late.
How buoyant we'd be
upon our return: our crew
of four highschoolers
and eight migrant workers
some as old as our fathers.
All of us tired the same,
all of us filthy the same,
fingernails, teeth, faces
all tempered with field grit
now half made of stone.

No.
There's a stitch in that stone,
in how giddy we are, giddy
and hungry these nights at
the end of our long drive home.
Rather like butterflies,
the last wave of monarchs
who were borne en route
over flyover states
on wings that inherited
a never-known path
to a single sacred tree
in Michoacan—
we arrived in Poynette
to a game that we played
as if never played before . . .
We ride into town near
sunset, looking for Wilbur.
We're looking for Wilbur
out front on his porch,
where the old man jokes
"I'll sit 'til the day I die,
and, who knows, maybe
a few days after."

So here we come,
a vanload of eyeballs,
and there he appears
in painter's pale coveralls.

The game begins:
A honk of the van horn
and our twenty-four hands
fly high in the windows,   *"How long's*
Honk, honk, wave, wave . . .   *your dong*
                                              Wilbur?"

        Our chorus sung low
        to be heard by us singers
        but unheard by Wilbur.   *"How long's*
        Honk, honk, wave, wave . . .   *your dong*
                                              Wilbur?"

        And reliably then—like doves
        in marbled light—both hands,
        Wilbur's hands in response
        fly over his shoulders
        at shoulder-width, so
        in his meaning to be
        waving *Hello, men! Hello!*
        he's also unwittingly
        answering *This long!*
        This long! to the lot of us,
        with whom this play plies
        every thread of animal
        delight, we whose laughter
        would flutter on forever . . .
        as we joyously reshaped
        ourselves the following day,
        and the day thereafter,
        and the day thereafter that,
        that summer crew,
        we who figured (quite
        correctly) that with
        a stroke of such "genius"
        we would never be
        the same again. We would
        never be the same again.

White Mountain Song

What the white whale was to Ahab has been
hinted; what, at times, he was to me, as yet
remains unsaid.

Honeymooners, hand in hand in swimsuits
we spacewalked in the sound pool awhile,
pale limbs humming to the tune of a whale
(a recording) moaning its eternal tones
to god-knows-whom about god-knows-what.
On that May afternoon in Pré-Saint-Didier
the only bummer was the overcast sky,
its white rotunda tie-dyed gray.
Mont Blanc, I'm afraid, is invisible today.
That detail aside, this was paradise.

Imagine: cetacean *Ees* and *Ohs*
that once spanned the ocean just once
now bubbled up to underwater ears, ours,
through Bose brand underwater speakers,
a singer—or was it two?—calling, calling
in perpetuity. *Isn't vhale song de vorld's*
most pure? In daht it lahdgely goes unheard
by humankind? I'd heard a German accent
ask this in English at the granola buffet,
and so floating there listening, I tried
my human hand at hearing. Mostly hearing
my wonder what the whale song means.
Surely something. Maybe *Ho there, dreamers.*
Ho there, lovers. Come, come climb

the slopes of this dream. Come, come climb
these clouds to the great white peak!—
or something of the sort.

For our part, Anna Belle, we played at forgetting
to remember: "It's our honeymoon, Honey!"
"How long have we been married now?"
"Two days." "Nope: two days and one hour."
Then later: "Two days, seven hours
and twenty-seven minutes" and so on.

      But how small
       it sounds

            to sing
           one's own.

A Roman and a Huguenot, both Americans,
water pillows cradling our newborn necks,
noodle floaties pillowing our newlywed knees,
our noses and eyelids chilly
in the springtime Piedmont air, so crisp.
You could even pretend we belong to this place
as we floated together, head to toe to head,
tracing the cycle of our one royal season
in that alpine thermal pool cooled to perfection—
meaning warmed in the belly of the Earth
then cooled to the temperature of skin,
the whole world made to feel just like our skin.

         But where
         oh where
         was The Mountain?

Where, for that matter, is any worthy
melody in our first luxury spa experience?

Though by no means exceptional,
I'm pretty sure we got the gist: you do your best
to do nothing at all. Like waves, our bodies
in the waters of the sky, we let bushel loads
of cumulus roll against the foothills, gathering
in mounds around the promise of a peak.
As our whale sang a song of The Mountain
we let the Earth spin as slowly as it pleased.
Overhead, under-toe, the White Mountain
out there, lost like a schooner, drifted
around the sky, as the two of us
—clock hands—floated in circular sound.

     But this song?
     What does it signify?

The next morning, day three, sunrise—voilà!
Awake early, I stood on the balcony naked as the blue
and beheld the great pale brow: Monte Bianco . . .
Oh I skipped over part of the story:
Two days earlier, wholly uninvited, a Milanese woman
had offered this reflection: "*E strano* Americani
to visit Val d'Aosta on moon of honey"—
True: we saw no other American tourists
(I first wrote *terrorists*) at the spa.
We heard not a word of English beyond our own.
Well except those Germans at breakfast.
Still, as I stood on the balcony that morning
I wondered for an unforgotten moment
back to that uninvited declaration:

     Strano . . . Strano. Why so *strange*?
     Strange in what sense? And, as if sprung
     from the seeds of such questions, a cosmos

of directionless wonders then wound
around my mind. Here's two examples:

One: I recalled that young American novelist
who's enraged by a second American novelist
who indeed turned a profit on a Holocaust tale
with nary a modicum of insight or grace.
The pair—both my acquaintances—had never met.
Then the mountain interrupted: "Well, first thing, Caligula,
you introduce these men as if both were your cousins.
Praise each, such extraordinary Republicans!
Do so publicly with sweeping Ciceronian flair . . .
Then discreetly sentence both to death."

And two: I recalled the following rhyme
composed by a man who'd rhymed so often
he never noticed that poets no longer rhyme:
Forgive, O Lord, my little jokes on Thee,
and I'll forgive Thy great big one on me.
This time the mountain responded with cheer:
"Ho, ho, there, Bei Dao! You return at last
to heed my call to sacrifice your son?"

Thereafter the valley air resounded
no signal—apart from songbird babble—
and I said nothing, knowing not what to say,
what rejoinder to The Mountain: I'm no Caligula?
Or, Who's Bei Dao? (I didn't know at the time
and I've since learned Bei Dao had no son.)
And there it ended, The White Mountain Song.

When I awakened you with flutes of champagne
that morning, you announced in jest—I think in jest—
"Married life has already started to wear on me."
Then next I recall we were back in the Fiat,

46

our bodies ever expanding in that tiny car,
its engine breathless on the foothill switchbacks.
The farther I drove up the valley, the farther
you leaned across the dash to catch the view.

While I guided our tires along the cliffs
you leaned out your window remarking at all
that I couldn't see: "There!" you said "Whoa!"
and so began to intone—though I'm sure
you didn't notice—this odd little song:

> *White . . . Blind . . . Switzerland . . . Permanent . . .*
> *There the lift car . . . Flying . . . Ice . . . What birds are . . .*
> *Switzerland . . . Whoa . . . Huge just . . . So . . .*

Words whose drums are especially hollow
from time to time sound the deepest boom,
our story so scattered it loses its tune.
We might have thought to wonder
what story was lost in the song,
but by then, love, we'd entered the tunnel
and our faces were flickering: blue, blue, blue.

That drive through the great Mont Blanc was peculiar:
I was actually *inside* the thing. We were *inside* together.
This alone is a wonder, an engineering wonder,
the sort of thing to which you know
you'll have to give more thought later.
But I'll tell you one thing:
not even Shelley got so close to the heart.

The New World

story tells *Who.*

story, the   Who?

carries a   If wind

If wind   is wind

Who?   only,

Who

went

the

way

of

the

wind.

American Homeric

What a shame. We used to begin *Sing, Muse!* But now we sing
    What a shame. So, not unlike Odysseus, the Homers head for

home. A shame then while forging the bog, most of the Homers
    succumb to mud inhalation. Those surviving few bubble up

shore-side with skin reminiscent of stone. The stone still sings.
    A shame that en route the stone-skinned poets forget their

essential shame—and forget more generally how things are
    and always have been, if you know what I mean. The stone

still sings. Arriving triumphal at the sea, the stony Homers
    construct a peninsula. They sing and they build 'til the reaches

are an isthmus conjoining the continents. A shame to reshape
    land in the image of man, don't you think? The stone still sings.

Like the gods we'd rather forget, it's a shame how predictably
    Homers sing only of Homers. A shame how people fall for that.

The stone still sings. Now, can't we agree, once and for all: forget
    those old Homers. A shame then, how we're hanging those poets

as statues in our plazas. The stone still sings. A shame to even
    be tickled by shadows of their limestone quills as we break in

to deface them with spray paint. We're too late. By now the song
    rings in outer space. But at last we hold the moon to account

for its stony disposition. Some say the stars are really stones.
    Homers. It's a shame how we fight about the stoniness of stars.

The stone still sings. A shame that no good could be cut from
    the stone out of which some Homer cut a song. But knowing

the stone must be cracked for the seed to catch fire, we crack
    that stone. Only now we recall that the last yellow rattle seed

sits in a jar in Miss Dilly's cellar, preserved—for our own good—
    lest that seed become the song the stone sings. What a shame.

IV

But, I take it, if he had genuine knowledge of the things he imitates he would far rather devote himself to real things than to the imitation of them, and would endeavor to leave after him many noble deeds and works as memorials of himself, and would be more eager to be the theme of praise, than the praiser.

- but -

Then felt I like some watcher of the skies
When a new planet swims into his ken;
Or like stout Cortez when with eagle eyes
He star'd at the Pacific—and all his men
Look'd at each other with a wild surmise—
Silent, upon a peak in Darien.

- but -

The signal waves of meaning vanish, having completed their work; the more potent they are, the more yielding, and the less inclined to linger.

- but -

King: *I have a dream.*

- but -

Revolutionary Word

Word, if you merely ring with truth, your truth, and nothing but your truth, you're already twice dead, and the thrice will bust the block for a chance to purchase you. Never delude yourself in belief that the heft of your being outweighs the candies of our president's imagination. Emulate instead the barns moaning and the air howling at the moment that afternoon sky let slip its black hole. Be only so material as the clef of the silver-throated crane, appearing (if we're so lucky) maybe twice and only in the least sacred places. Like the parking lot of the Walgreens on Prospect Ave. And when you alight, Word, then spring aloft at once, just as that sandhill I saw landed then was up and gone in the sky above the Del Monte cabbage plant. A poignancy that could easily be mistaken for a body. Visit only where no crowd can gather. Then, Word, what can you say? Not a rhetorical *What can you say*. What can you say to embody not only what arrived iridescent but what endures with the wherewithal of wasps? With savor as your only song, and filament your only tower, be the last human feather to fall to earthly power.

In Exodus

A comet tail marking the pre-dawn dark,
the speedometer needle brushes 70.
The radioactive cosmos of the dial
glazes my knuckles green along the wheel.
The two of us, road-tripping, westward ho!
Our eyes laze along the penumbral scrawls
of barn tops, a rip-tooth of peaks breaking up
from the loam. It's Hart Crane's New York skyline
inverted here in the caves of the past—
in the deep heart of Pennsylvania, I mean.

Hey babe, let's put on some Dylan
I almost say, but never get the chance . . .

                    thunderhead-grand at the end of the Earth
                    the leaden lid of the eye of Apollo
Day-   has begun to draw back, opening.
break: The stare from the sky we face explodes
                    down the sluice of Interstate 80,
                    redrawing the lanes of our one given path.

So of course we can't see a thing.
Marvelous as it may sound, as it may be,
to steer your lover along an arc to eternity,
all we see is the sun-resplendent prism
of windshield bugs, their jeweled guts.
Gross. One wonders what wonders one

misses as into this necklace of moments—
when, for example, you hand me my shades;
and, later, when I re-grip the wheel with all
the care of a novice cosmonaut, hands 10 and 2;
and, later still, whenever the sun delivers
its punch line—this ancient image falls.

That our biblical selves are jumping the queue,
residues, Abrahams: one in me, one in you . . .
That it takes years to even begin to decode
these lingerings. (Really, *what* goes on here?)
That it's just a spell of highway hypnosis, suppose,
this backward loop we ride, this loop ad infinitum:
that the road is a road back to memory first
then a road back to you, here, now.

What would it be   as one may some-
to sail into memory   times in a moment
gracefully back   gracefully forth?

In recalling the mountain that is lost
and stepping through and stepping well
may we, at times, rebound through time
as knights of faith in the land of milk and honey?

One floats like this in exodus
from time to time. One can't not somer-
sault out into space from the ship of
the stories we've been told and mis-
told. We misinhabit so many worlds
at once: all of us exiles once, all of us
migrant, all of us slaves, arriving
in this heartland, land of steel and coal.
No, no: not *all* of us slaves, not in this desert.

Who is surprised   Who is surprised
when this vision dies   when a new vision rises
in no time at all?   to be reckoned?

Here in the Prius, you hit play on the disc *Desire*
then recline for a 7 a.m. nap. Today's sun is odd—
have you noticed?—an oddity our poet orders
but our pilgrim passes unawares, ballooning ahead
over silos to the west, all silhouettes. Un-blinded
in my Ray-Ban shades with one lens cracked,
I will drive us to Toledo, then on to South Bend,
then toward Gary, the home of the Jackson Five,
the city poised to be our most resplendent ruins.

A future unfolds more clearly than a past:
that we know we break for a second coffee soon,
that we fill the tank twice more with flight fuel,
that we grab subs, maybe burritos at an Indiana wayside—
we've tried both joints before. They're pretty good . . .

All I say to you is "Sweet dreams, love."—but also:
that we never speak of the featureless stretches
of cultivated land: oats, wheat, soybeans, tobacco;
that most go missing in any given read. For example
that I miss the roadside crucifix, tall as a radio tower,
though I've seen it before; also the pink elephant
standing outside Citgo sporting spectacles. Presently
I almost miss the life and times of an in-between farm,
what people now call a "family farm," its barn
backed up to the highway, its once bright blood walls
pale and buckling, its six heifers serene in the steam
of the low manured corner of the pasture
on any cool morning such as this,

for, concurrently, I wonder: might it not be
that you whose faith will someday save me,
that you, back looping in dreams, have just
returned to me by today's celestial anomaly
with your shoelaces galaxied in honeycomb,
and it's for this reason, love, (and not
the odoriferous emanations of the cow dung,)
that you, right now, lift your head and wonder aloud:
"Hey, do you smell that? It's . . . something . . . sweet."

Osip in August

There was Osip, as there was a photograph I lost, I remember better now.
As there is a bird and a wolf and a black foil path running back to old

songs. As those songs that even the singer never heard I remember.
As while out on coffee break this morning, we saw the poet Mandelstam

and didn't skip a beat. There was Osip, older than he ever lived to be,
staring at his hands held up cupping sunlight. As one happens to know

though the world disconforms to the poem, the poet's arrival is perfectly
natural, even inevitable—so wholly so that we barely notice. As an iced

latte is just so delicious. As, only later, as these appearances germinate,
I begin to see what I saw. As I recall the geometer of empty Arabian sands.

As I hear the train's whistle and prescient whispers of a Primus stove.
As I see the great mustache. As I'm astonished to see Osip older, balder,

shorter than one judges from the last photo. As outside Café Regular,
he stood statue-still on the sidewalk, paying no heed as we passed

with our coffees in hand. As one click earlier, awaiting our lattes,
I had misremembered and so had misquoted and then I corrected

(so I thought) one of Osip's exquisite lines. *It was sound*, I said, *not
light pouring into the fingers of mortals. But I,* Osip wrote, *I have*

forgotten what I wanted to say. My friend, did you notice the old man
praying in the street? As the moment remembers me reciprocally

I remember the hand made of worms and the arms of a clock face
turning in a treetop; I recall that, at the end of December of 1938,

at an uncertain hour, Mandelstam dies; the poet skips off o'er a chance
path of junk boats aligned just this once in the mist; I recall these facts

have arisen from a fiction. As the photo I remember is the path curving
back to silver songs. As there's that tiny double portrait of the poet:

one front-facing and the second shot in profile, images I lifted today
from the curb, where they drop like sparrow wings, separate and askew.

Who drops them? What brother of Osip has just passed by? As the ages
rush around in their infinite uniforms, no two the same, I return

to Moscow quiet as a coffin. As Osip's woolen suit is too heavy for
the season, how his sleeves were striped in sweat and wrinkled

like sun-ruined skin. As I remember his hands held up to his chin, up
and palms together. As he bows in close to the pages, as if his verses

have been puzzled by time, transmogrified to tongues (like English)
wholly unknown to the poet. As like death, in time the portraits become

irresistible, as half of Osip's feathers are broken or missing. As the poor
man's feathers are broken or missing and thereafter the story is born.

As even across eighty winters, in one glance you've recited the story
in full, and the image itself is somehow now soothed for the moment,

as a lost child held by a stranger in a crowd. As already a nomad—
or exile, rather—he's banished to the east, then re-banished further.

As in Vladivostok, in the midway of his life, he dies of ice and failure,
or so the story goes. As in the last photograph he appears much older

than a man of forty-seven, though not half as old as he appears to us today. *But I,* Osip writes, *I've forgotten what I wanted to say.* As this

was Osip in 1920, then our cold drinks appeared on the counter and we carried them out. As we entered the painted unparticular fortress

of that Brooklyn street, over-domed by London plane trees, bastioned by ivied townhouses, and busy only with the towheaded kiddos

who flash downhill on their scooters. And there was the pilgrim. And there a bird and a wolf and a stone. As here's the poem: it's the ruins,

not the fortress we recall and recite. Not the fortress but the stones we trip over on land we mistook for untouched. That here the earth

spits up time's architecture, the stone footings of our proper sorrow. Here are the holes in the hands that we build and rebuild to forget

what's lost. That that was Osip we circled, so as not to awaken a man so enthralled. That that was Osip as we parted and swallowed

the seas to the right and left of his body; that that was Osip recalled by misremembered verses; that the bird and the wolf are still here

patient in the roar of the moment. And that it is sound, finally, not light pouring into his fingers; it is sound not light pouring into our fingers.

That it's the songbird elegizing Osip today; and that it is us, friend, stepping these immortal steps away, I remember better now.

Fire Watcher

A simple idea: a tower built taller
than the trees on the hill, a full head higher,
so one standing guard can see a little farther,

see strikes and the sparks of lightning,
spot the first line of smoke far off in the bluffs,
feel the wind above all, listen to its hinting,

then call out a warning to the village below . . .
The young man listens for the moment—
the right moment—to speak of

the tower he carries as a word and place,
a lost place, a trouble. Its lookout was empty
at the end of a hundred airy stairs.

Alone a moment in the cage in the sky,
a boy then, he climbed up ahead of his father
and so arrived there unknowing

before he arrived. The wind was stronger
as his father still climbed. The moment
was closer when his father arrived

behind him. Then he lifted him higher
to clear the rail and chain link
to see the pine treetops cushioning off

down the hill. There below was a scoop
in the green, a fenced-in clearing of sickly
looking grass, paper bag brown. In that burn

were bison, two big and one small—
now the three of them tiny and tinier still.
The mechanical beasts in clouds of drought

had shot them an eye when they approached
from the truck. Still held now he listens
for the moment to speak of the tower,

but what can he tell? Up there together
for hours on end in a four-year-old's time
his father lifted him up for a view.

He thinks what he said was: "Now look
at the treeline, do you see any trailings?
Do you see any storms, or lightning, or fire?

Behind us? Look over there under the sun.
Be patient. It's the fire watcher's gift,
patience." With shoe toes pinched

in the chain link squares, he looked and
he looked as a man should. All around
with his father in the cage in the sky

he looked like a hawk on the treetops
and down the slow slopes to the village
where they lived. He's looking like this

for the moment to speak of the tower
he carries within him—now for how
many years? How wind there is stronger

and the moment is closer. He knew
what to look for, how he wanted so wholly
to see there the wisps of a word,

the first sign of fire. He knew, just so,
how the smoke should appear,
for this was a fact as true as the hands

of his father behind him, how its billows
would shadow the bright, brighten
the shadow, and lean to the left

bent off in the wind. Left, he knew,
for the wind on his face was the wind
in the sky, this same wind. It seems

only now that that hour is closer:
the word, and the place, the lost place,
the trouble; that he was the end

of a line of fire watchers,
and he'd arrived too late to the post,
the tower unmanned in a time of fire,

fire as emissary, fire as order, fire as teacher,
the new world fire. There's no one
up there watching, to be sure.

The tower was taller than the trees
on the hill, a full head higher, so the one
sitting guard would see a little farther,

now it's a skinless giant with wind flaming
through, an empty curiosity only.
The young man is curious, still.

Old Lines

> *. . . if he has lived sincerely, it must have been in a*
> *distant land to me. Perhaps these pages are more*
> *particularly addressed to poor students.*

> —Henry David Thoreau

I shouldn't even look.
The fifteen hundred pheasants lit on the field are stuck in cages
as they have been every year.

A field east of town is set aside for game birds, nets
draped over wood trusses, posts and crossbars stained bark gray.
I tell you, Pilgrim, something's wrong.

These eyes.
Some mornings the light driving down
deliberate on the acres of fabric has convinced me of fog.

Fog, I think, and this familiar peace rolls through me all day.
Tricks. It's the light.
The same sun in the evenings will color everything
with a richness I can't explain.
No.
There's nothing like it in old paintings, nothing like it in foreign lands.

Last night, over my drive home
the sky was unimaginable, cloudscape, thin moon.
The land around the highway darkened,
expected, to the wooded corners of the clearing.

On these nights, when I pass the pheasant field, I've come to expect it
—a moment when I miss the nets washed out
by this particular trick
of light, and the painted birds
emerge, out there, unfettered, simply waiting

—McIntoshes—fifty acres scattered with apples.
I'm certain of it. This is not our place.
I mean the world.

Notes

3   The Plato quote is from *Republic*, Book X, translated by Paul Shorey.

15   Especially among the people of India, "26/11" refers to the day on which the city of Mumbai was attacked by members of Lashkar-e-Taiba.

15   The "sigh" and "*ages and ages hence*" are from Robert Frost's poem "The Road Not Taken."

19   Any grace in this translation of Osip Mandelstam's "Octet 9" is due to the insights of Amy Hosig and Leeore Schnairsohn.

27   The Keats is from "Upon First Looking into Chapman's Homer."

36   Note 1: This poem remembers an episode at the end of Canto XX in Dante's *Purgatorio*. Charles Singleton's prose translation of the epigraph is as follows: "No ignorance—if my memory err not in this—did ever with so great assault make me desirous of knowing as it seemed I then experienced in thought." Note 2: In his sonnet "Upon First Looking into Chapman's Homer," John Keats places Hernán Cortéz on a mountaintop in Panama, glimpsing the Pacific Ocean for the first time. In fact, that explorer could only have been Vasco Núñez de Balboa. The mistake was pointed out to Keats, but he chose not to correct it—presumably because the extra syllable in the name "Balboa" would unbalance the sonnet's ten-syllable line.

37   The Mandelstam is from "Conversation about Dante," translated by Jane Gary Harris and Constance Link.

43   Epigraph from *Moby-Dick*, Chapter 42.

46   Italicized lines are a couplet recited by Robert Frost.

51   Dr. Martin Luther King Jr. gave this speech on August 28, 1963.

54   The expression "rip-tooth" is from Hart Crane's "Proem: To Brooklyn Bridge."

64   These lines appeared earlier in *Carnations* and earlier than that in *Washington Square*. The epigraph and italicized line are both from *Walden*.

PRINCETON SERIES OF CONTEMPORARY POETS